BABY TAMING

BABY TAMING

by Peter Mayle / Illustrated by Arthur Robins

H·A·R·M·O·N·Y B·O·O·K·S

New York

This book is for my mother and father, and about time too.

Published simultaneously in Canada by General Publishing Co., Ltd.
Printed in the United States of America.

Library of Congress Cataloging in Publication Data

Mayle, Peter.
Baby taming.
1. Children—Management.   2. Children—Management—Anecdotes, facetiae, satire, etc.
I. Title.
HQ769. M377   1978   649'.1   78-15532
ISBN 0-517-53534-3

10   9   8   7   6   5   4

Invasion by a Small but Cunning Enemy

I have a sneaking fondness for babies, even after five of my own.

I understand why they enjoy a reputation for being fascinating, charming, lovable, and cuddly. They deserve it. All the babies of my acquaintance have had those

qualities in abundance. Why do you think movie stars never want to work with them?

As if that weren't enough, babies are also blessed with astonishing organizational abilities. How they did it from their cribs I'll never know, but they have managed to set up the world's most successful and long-running public relations campaign.

More insidious and effective than anything the CIA could dream up, this worldwide conspiracy has been operating against unsuspecting men and women for years. Encouraged by big business, the pediatric branch of the medical profession, organized religion, and umpteen million grandparents, we are led to believe that the arrival of a baby is a joyous and carefree event. More than that. We are promised that it will add another dimension to our lives.

So it does, but not the one that's advertised.

Babies are not the helpless, innocent creatures they appear to be. Beneath that wrinkled, rosy exterior lurk the mind and instincts of a seasoned guerilla fighter, determined to force you, the parent, into unconditional surrender. No holds are barred, no weapon too ghastly to be used against you. Predawn attacks are commonplace; assaults with loaded diapers and ear-piercing battle cries are just the beginning of the struggle.

But what is the war about? What does the little monster want? Just this: your total and unquestioning obedience to every gurgle and yell; the rearrangement of your entire life to suit his or her schedule; and twenty-four-hour attention. During the first year, your baby will try to lay the foundations for a whole childhood of making you jump. You have only to look at other people's children to see how successful this strategy can be.

In the chapters that follow, we will take you through the tactics, secret weapons, booby traps, and ambushes that have defeated parents in the past. We will show you how to recognize the signs of an impending diaper attack, how to foil

bogus bedtime tantrums, how to pace yourself through the struggle, and how to fight back, using techniques and equipment that have been combat-tested in bedroom, bathroom and high chair.

With the exception of the next chapter, all the information is arranged by subject rather than by chronological age. The reason for this is that babies never seem to do what they're supposed to do when they're supposed to do it. Teeth can appear at birth, or at eighteen months; the same with hair. Elementary toilet training and table manners can take months or years. Some babies walk at nine months; others prefer to crawl until they're two.

All this, as you will find, is part of a baby master plan designed to confuse you and keep you off balance. We don't want to add to the confusion by telling you to expect certain stages of development to happen at precise ages.

Having said that, there is one age where you *can* expect to notice a certain pattern of behavior: the first three months of life. (Some people call this the Golden Age, but they're wrong. Children are at their best from age twenty-one onwards.) These early months may seem peaceful, and indeed they often are, but beware. This whole period is but the first in a series of shameless deceptions, as we are about to see.

The Phony Truce

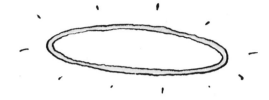

All babies come into the world equipped with an instinctive tactical sense and an uncanny ability to conceal their real intentions. This is true even during the first three months of life.

During that time, while they are gathering their strength and studying your weaknesses, they are quiet, tractable, and utterly disarming. Apart from the inconvenient mealtimes and the occasional bout of indigestion, you would hardly know you have a baby in the house. All those tales you hear about other people's little demons may be true, but your baby isn't like that. Your baby is different.

If you believe that, you've already lost the first battle of the war.

The peace of those first three months is a deliberate maneuver to lull you into dropping your guard. It is baby's first bluff, and nine times out of ten it works. When war is eventually declared, and your angel turns into a screaming savage, you are taken completely by surprise.

Like all bluffs, though, it can be called. While this period of calm lasts, you can take advantage of your superior size, weight, and speed to introduce the early stages of feeding, potting, and bathing routines that we suggest later on. Don't wait until your baby is "old enough to understand"; by then it's too late. This first three months offers literally the chance of a lifetime. Don't miss it.

Baby's Headquarters

The most basic requirement for baby taming, apart from an iron will, is a properly fitted room—one in which toys can be stored, diapers can be changed, and tempers left to cool off. And the more interesting you can make this room, the happier your baby will be to spend time there.

All babies love color and movement, and will begin to respond to them when only a few weeks old. The more you can make their immediate environment resemble an overloaded Christmas tree, the better they'll like it. Save your aesthetic standards for the rest of the house. The baby's room should be festooned with things that move, tinkle, shine, and reflect. Mobiles, bells, mirrors, musical boxes, plants, goldfish in their bowls, birds in their cages—whatever you can cram into the space. It is impossible to have too much going on.

Ideally, you'll have a changing table in the same room; and since the average baby goes through between five and six thousand diapers, it makes sense to have a table that is designed or adapted for the job. Get one that is a comfortable height (most tables are too low) and

have a couple of washable foam-rubber pads cut to fit it. You might also want to fix up a padded strap to anchor the baby so you have both hands free. And while you're at it, hang a mobile directly over the table. If there's something to look at up above, it helps to distract the baby from doing any serious squirming.

Now, before you have to, is a good time to child-proof the windows and make sure the door can't be locked accidentally (or on purpose) from the inside. This should be the one room in the house where you know that a few minutes' silence isn't the prelude to a disaster.

As the months go by, the room will change. You'll need bookshelves, a low table and chair, and a storage place for toys.

We've found the normal toy box quite useless; whatever you're looking for is always at the bottom. The ideal container is something like a low trough with several compartments—one for blocks, one for soft toys, and so on. It doesn't matter if the toys get mixed up. They'll still be a lot easier to find than if they were in a regular box. (A minor consideration? You wait until you hear the furious yells of a baby whose teddy bear has gone AWOL in the bottom of a crowded box.)

The Breast and the Bottle

Nowadays, doctors and hospitals are strongly recommending breast feeding, but it is obviously your decision. Here are the main pros and cons.

Nature provides most mothers with enough milk to feed a baby for approximately six months. It's free, it's digestible, and there is no special equipment needed to prepare it or bring it to the correct temperature. It's the ideal food—until you start to consider the snags.

There are several potential problems, from painful nipples to an excess of milk. But nothing is quite as alarming as the thought that *you can never take a weekend off.* Worse than that, you can't even skip one meal. Husbands can't help. Baby-sitters don't have the natural resources. The baby has you in a corner, and there you'll stay for months. No wonder the world is taking to the bottle.

A High-decibel Bedtime Program

Perhaps the inside of a womb is a very noisy spot; perhaps a newborn baby's hearing isn't all that acute. Whatever the reason, babies are born with the capability of sleeping through just about anything short of a direct bomb attack. This priceless attribute should be encouraged from the very first week at home.

Make it a habit to turn the hi-fi up, not down, at bedtime. Stop tiptoeing around. With sufficient conditioning, a baby could be placed in the middle of the Boston Symphony Orchestra and still get a good night's sleep.

On the other hand, if you encourage the practice of whispers and perfect peace at bedtime, the slightest noise will be enough to wake your baby, disturb your cocktail hour, and ruin your dinner. It's up to you.

Submerging Your Baby

Most babies *like* water. They bob around in amniotic fluid for the best part of nine months, so they are accustomed to the sensation of floating. Before this wears off and they find their land legs, they should be introduced to the daily bath during their first few days at home.

At first, your baby may pretend not to like it. (To be fair, going from the womb to a bath must feel like leaving the backyard pool for the Atlantic.) But it's worth persevering. If you can get your baby used to the bath at this early age, when screams are pitched at minimum volume, you will save yourself hours of bad-tempered and soapy wrestling in the months to come.

Be prepared for one particular trouble spot; most babies hate to be shampooed—an early sign of the instinctive desire to cling onto as much of the day's dirt as possible. If this is the case with your baby, keep a small mirror next to the bath and see if this sequence of events works for you the same way that it did for us:

1. Wet the baby's head (screams). 2. Apply the shampoo (more screams). 3. Coax the hair, such as it is, into horns, curls, wings or whatever else you can manage quickly. 4. Show baby your handiwork in the mirror.

At worst, this will probably reduce the baby to an astonished silence, while the apparition in the mirror is studied. At best, your baby will adore the shampoo game and look forward to the next time. Either way, the hair gets washed. You win.

The Invisible Umbilical Cord

Babies are experts at giving you the impression of total helplessness. One slightly cross-eyed glance is enough to convince most

new parents that it would be heartless and irresponsible to leave their little darling alone for an instant.

Mothers especially, be on your guard. This is a psychological extension of the umbilical cord, and for everyone's sake it is best cut young. It's difficult to exercise any restraint during the first few weeks, because babies are the most engaging and fascinating toys ever invented. This, of course, is something they know very well. Rule number one in the baby combat manual states: "If you can fake them out for the first three months, you can fake them out for life." Remember that rule every time you're tempted to sit adoringly by the bedside instead of going into the living room and having a drink.

The baby who becomes used to sharing every moment with you ends up demanding nonstop attention. The baby who becomes used to sharing your bedroom develops chronic and noisy insomnia when asked to sleep alone. It's that simple. Babies expect what you teach them to expect.

Baby Talk vs. English

Babies, like puppies, respond to intonation rather than the specific word. You can say "good girl" and produce a smile or tears depending on how you say it.

Since the word itself is less important than how it's spoken, it is hard to understand the popularity of the gibberish that passes for communication between some parents and their offspring. If a baby can comprehend beddy-byes, bathy-poo and breky-weky, surely bed, bath and breakfast would sink in just as easily.

The obvious advantages of speaking English to your baby from the word go are that you have to teach only one vocabulary, and your baby has to learn only one language. You also avoid the humiliation that occurs when an obstinate and evil-minded baby insists on being addressed in baby talk in public.

Eat, Drink, and Be Messy

Most babies feel that they can score important victories during mealtimes. Apart from the sensual delights of running their fingers through their lunch, there are plenty of opportunities to wear you down with a variety of sticky and unpleasant surprise attacks. If none of these tactics works, there is always the ultimate threat of refusing to eat and dying of self-induced starvation.

The less you need to worry about accidental spills or deliberate sabotage the better. The ideal feeding area is a car wash, or a small tiled cell that can be hosed down after each meal. Failing that, choose a corner of the kitchen as far away as possible from appliances, delicate plants, and the dog's basket. Get your baby used to wearing a pelican bib (the kind that catches most of the food falling from the mouth). And make sure that you yourself are dressed for the occasion.

A protective garment that covers you from throat to knee is best—something like a smock. There are plenty of things *not* to wear, like silk shirts, cashmere sweaters, fragile jewelry, and watches that aren't food-proof. Keep a couple of reserve feeding spoons, a box of tissues, a small mirror and a damp washcloth within arm's reach. These will come in handy when you are faced with baby's favorite diversionary tactics, such as:

1. Mouth Open, also known as the cement-mixer game. As the food goes into the mouth, it

is turned over once or twice by the tongue before being vigorously ejected.

Counterattack: Withdraw the food and apply damp washcloth. Pretend to be busy with something else for a few minutes. Baby will be puzzled, then suspicious, then bored. Now's the moment to try another spoonful. If that succeeds, resume feeding. If not, don't waste your time. Your baby isn't hungry.

2. Mouth Closed in the "my lips are sealed" position. Neither spoon nor mug nor nipple shall pass.

Counterattack: Short of pinching the nostrils together, the best way to get the mouth open is to feed from above, since upward movement of head often leads to downward movement of lower jaw. The mirror is also useful here; babies love to watch themselves eat.

3. Floor-bombing, direct attacks on you, and attempts at mid-air interception of your feeding hand with a flying fist are often used all at once, like a boxer's combination of punches.

Counterattack: Chances are that this is temper and not playfulness. You can try holding both your baby's hands with your free hand, but this usually only works while the surprise lasts. Next, try a spoonful from above, then one from the back, then from below. If your footwork is dazzling enough, your baby will be too busy watching you to reject the food.

4. The Food-as-a-Hat Trick. Very popular with babies as a tour de force if lesser tactics haven't worked. Either a handful of food or the whole plateful is deposited in the hair and massaged firmly into the roots, usually while you're on the phone.

Counterattack: Tight-fitting rubber hats and instant sponge-downs are both unpopular, and often cause hysterics. If you can bear it, just let the little beast sit there until discomfort sets in. Otherwise, proceed directly to bath-time.

Of course, you may not feel like indulging

your baby even to the extent we suggest. Fair enough. If you're prepared to be firm, there's no reason that you shouldn't preside over quiet and well-ordered meals.

Good eating habits are the direct result of good feeding habits. For example, allocate a certain amount of time to each feed (ten minutes, twenty minutes, whatever your patience will stand). At the end of that time, clear the food away. Don't worry if all of it hasn't been eaten. When babies are hungry, they eat. Playing with the last few mouthfuls is simply another delaying tactic, designed to sap your patience and willpower.

Don't turn meals into spectator sports by letting friends and neighbors watch your baby eat. That's exactly what the little devil wants, and will play up to the gallery with at least one trick from the disgusting repertoire listed above. If you make meals into special events, you can hardly blame your baby for doing the same.

Except in extraordinary circumstances, try to stick to the same times each day for feeding. There is a school of thought that favors feeding on demand, which will very quickly make your life hell. It's up to you to set the mealtimes; baby's appetite and digestive system will fit in with your timetable after the first few weeks.

Inevitably, the day will come when your baby will want to dispense with your services and feed itself. A mixed blessing. It involves even more mess in the early stages, and mealtimes will take longer. But at least it gets you off the hook to a certain extent. Be warned, though. Baby will try to enlist you as an appreciative audience for the wonders of coordination which

will now be revealed. Don't fall for it. Place the high chair in an open, safe, easily washed-down area. Put baby, food, and drink in position, then *go away.* Otherwise you'll find that your presence is required before a single mouthful is eaten. Once the baby is used to self-feeding, social eating with the rest of the family can be tried.

A word about indigestion, which plagues most infants from birth to about five months. We recommend two positions: for normal postprandial burping, sit the baby upright. Place one hand on the stomach, the other at the base of the back. Work the hand at the baby's back all the way up to the shoulders with a circular motion, pressing the stomach gently with the other hand. For really stubborn four-star attacks of gas pain, lay the baby face down on your lap and use the same circular massage motion from the base of the back toward the shoulders. Don't forget to have a washcloth handy to catch the odd dribble.

Some Cleaning Instructions

abies are seldom halfhearted about taking a bath. They either hate it or love it; so you should be prepared for noisy resistance either getting in or getting out. As for hair washing, very few babies actually enjoy the process. (This is partly due to the sensation of being submerged, and partly due to a desire to hold on to those morsels of today's lunch which were so carefully massaged into the scalp.)

There are two general rules that we have found to be very effective in the bathroom.

The first, as we have already suggested, is to begin complete immersion at the earliest possible age—and that includes a daily shampoo or head-wetting.

The second is a secret weapon that most babies find completely irresistible, and which we are convinced is the world's best bath toy: you. If you can schedule your bath to coincide with the

baby's you'll find yourself able to carry out tricky cleaning jobs (hair, ears, etc.) while your baby is busy studying you. Of course, the novelty wears off eventually, but by then you've won. Your baby has missed the chance to get hysterical over those first shampoos, and you'll be able to treat any further displays of temperament with the firmness they deserve.

Grips and Techniques

The single-handed hold, the lap grip and the shampoo position are for basic everyday use. You will probably develop your own more imaginative variations as you get used to your baby's attempts to escape. Provided the head is fully supported at all times and the eyes are kept clear of soap and shampoo, any grip that works for you is fine.

The End of the Toothless Grin

It's not strictly fair to add teething to this collection of juvenile dirty tricks. This time, there's no faking or mischief involved; teething can really hurt. We've included it here because although it's not a deliberate ploy on your baby's part, it can still try your patience, disrupt your life, and interfere with the training process.

Some babies are lucky enough to cut a headful of teeth with no more than the occasional twinge; others go through hell with every tooth. The degree of discomfort varies enormously, like most aspects of teething.

You can't even predict with any kind of accuracy when the first tooth will arrive. Louis XIV was *born* with teeth—two of them. Many babies are toothless until well over a year old. Going by statistics, you can expect the first teeth to make an appearance some time between four and nine months.

If your baby is one of the unlucky ones fated to have a tough time, the signs of teething will be painfully easy to spot. They could be any or all of these: inflamed cheeks and gums, general grouchiness, a constant dribble, and an angry diaper rash.

Unfortunately, nothing you can do is going to prevent the discomfort entirely. You'll hear about, and probably try on your baby, all kinds of strange remedies, from rubbing vodka on the gums to chewing dog biscuits. Less exotic

pain relievers are easier to administer and more likely to work. Here's a short selection:

Teething Jellies

There are several to choose from. They all work in the same way, by coating the sore part of the gums with a very mild local anaesthetic. Flavors vary, so try two or three until you find a taste that suits your baby. Note: Don't rub the gums too hard with your fingers when applying the jelly; you could make them even more sore, or cause an infection.

Teething Biscuits

The harder they are, the more relief they seem to provide for those itching gums. The kind of biscuit that resists going soggy for the longest time is best; perhaps dog biscuits aren't such a weird idea after all. We've also heard good reports about stale bagels. One side benefit of teething biscuits is that in times of severe loss of appetite they can be the only solid food that passes your baby's lips.

Teething Rings

A standby for thousands of years. What used to be silver, ivory, or leather is nowadays rubber or plastic. There is a particularly ingenious kind available that has liquid sealed inside the ring; you keep it in the icebox until needed. This freezes the liquid and provides a marvelously soothing suck.

The Icebox

Extreme cold is bliss for sore gums. Keep in the icebox everything your baby regularly chews or sucks when it's not in use — teething rings, rusks, teething jelly, spoons, pacifiers, the works.

The Nightcap

Frowned on by some who see it as the first step on the road to ruin, a godsend to others, the occasional nightcap has been found to be harmless and helpful. A tot of whisky or brandy in the nighttime bottle has the same effect on babies that it does on adults. The pain is dulled, the world is a rosier place, and sleep is easier.

As if sore gums weren't enough, teething symptoms occur at the other end of the baby too. Diaper rash, caused mainly by bacteria, is aggravated by the extra-strong urine that accompanies teething. It must feel something like putting peroxide on a cut.

Without bacteria there wouldn't be a bad rash in the first place, so the cleaner the baby, the less chance of a rash. If, despite frequent diaper changes, a rash does develop, keep the sore skin well greased with petroleum jelly or Vitamin A + D Cream. And be sure to let some fresh air get to the rash. Let your baby go bottomless for as long as possible every day; it helps healing, and you can imagine how incredibly refreshing it must feel.

"The Only Good Baby Is a Sleeping Baby"

Babies are at their most appealing at bedtime; freshly bathed and full of after-supper charm. Is this a happy accident arranged by nature? Far from it. Babies *know* that your resistance is getting low at this hour of the day. They are aware that a well-aimed smile can delay bedtime for up to five minutes; two smiles and a gurgle, ten minutes; and one barely intelligible word is often good for half an hour, while you try to work out what your little genius was trying to say.

Roughly translated, the little genius was saying: "I am not ready to go to bed yet."

Babies are hams. They dread the moment when the light goes out and the audience disappears. At the slightest sign of encouragement they will perform with a professional smoothness that would do credit to the dolphins at Marineland.

Difficult though it is to bring an end to this performance, you must. Otherwise, like a junkie who can't shake the habit, you'll be hooked on charm, and your baby will know it. At the first sign of any disciplinary nonsense from you, the smiles, the dimples, and the gurgles will be turned on until you submit, a victim of the worst kind of subversive warfare. You won't even know you've lost until it's too late.

Don't weaken. If you've decided that bedtime is 6 o'clock, make sure you're sitting down with

THUD!

a drink at 6:05, and not dancing attendance at the bedside.

There is a price to pay before you can feel that victory is yours. As soon as your baby realizes that charm isn't going to work, less subtle weapons will be brought into play. For relatively small creatures, babies have supernaturally powerful lungs; you'll hear them at full blast for several nights.

These tantrums will not be just plain bellowing, although that will certainly form part of the act. Most babies are capable of expressing their outrage with a wide range of vocal effects, from a pathetic whimpering calculated to make your neighbors think you've been using thumbscrews and a bullwhip, all the way up to an express-train shriek, interspersed with heavy sighs, sobs and the occasional ominous thud.

The first time you hear this astounding performance, you are convinced something dreadful has happened—head stuck through the bars of the crib at the very least. You rush into the bedroom, petrified with worry and remorse—to be greeted by a tear-stained face wearing a broad grin. Miraculously, your baby turns the noise off and the charm on. You've lost.

The only thing to do is harden your heart, resign yourself to a half-hour of high-octane screeching for a week or so, and retire to the farthest corner of your house until baby gets bored and tired and gives up.

Sooner or later, your baby will probably develop a persistent bedtime passion for one particular object. It may be a doll, an old rubber pacifier, a piece of silk, a cotton handkerchief, a fur hat, a thumb, an old cotton diaper or a tattered blanket. The objects vary, but their purpose is the same: to provide comfort and soothing familiarity in times of tiredness and stress.

All that seems innocent enough. But you should know that these outwardly harmless odds and ends have a secondary purpose: they are there to get lost and cause you trouble. Once your baby has established that the sticky Barbie doll with one leg is essential for a good night's rest, you can be sure that it won't be long before the doll vanishes. Baby is broken-hearted. As bedtime approaches, panic sets in. No substitute will do. The whole household is turned upside down to look for the wretched doll, and bedtime is postponed until it's found. Which is, of course, exactly what your baby had in mind when hiding the doll under the mattress earlier in the day.

However bizarre the favorite pacifier is, be sure you have an identical replacement tucked away. If it means buying a brand-new doll and abusing it until it reaches the required state of scruffiness, go ahead. The time and money will be well spent.

One of the many shocks to the system that babies love to deliver will come at between 6—12 months. Just as you think you've got the whole bedtime problem licked, your baby will suddenly discover how to climb out of the crib. This is a crucial test of your ability to cope with unexpected combat conditions, because there's no telling when this moment will come.

Keep calm. Conceal your surprise. Don't exclaim over baby's new-found climbing talent. Don't make an event out of it by calling your

husband, wife or friends to have a look. Return the baby to bed *as if nothing had happened.* Baby will be mystified, having expected a much more dramatic reaction from you. The two or three days of puzzlement that follow will give you time to put new, higher bolts on the doors and windows, or to make arrangements to convert the playpen into a large and high-barred bed.

The Longest Battle of All

Entire books have been written about toilet training, but they ignore the subtleties of the situation. Much, much more is involved than teaching the mere mechanical process of using a pot instead of a diaper. Bluff and counterbluff, bribery and threat, will-power versus instinct—they all have their place in this long and often bitterly fought struggle.

The textbooks say that a child has little control over the bowels until the age of two, or the bladder until two and a half. This may be true, but we have our doubts. It's important to bear in mind from the start that babies are not dumb. It doesn't take them long to work out that a dirty, wet diaper is an uncomfortable place to spend the day. Neither does it take long for them to realize that they could be dry and comfortable if only they performed on demand and on the pot.

So why are they prepared to endure months or years of discomfort? Because they know full well that this is one of the best opportunities they'll ever get to impose their will on you. Everything is in their favor and, more or less, under their control. They can strike day or night. The element of surprise is always working for them. All this, they feel, is worth a few damp hours each day.

Toilet training is a war of attrition, and the side that succeeds in establishing a pattern will win. If you wait for your baby to make the first move, you're halfway toward losing. Take the initiative while you still can.

As soon as you feel that your baby is ready to sit up comfortably with support from you, get into a routine: five minutes on the pot immediately after every meal. You'll hear a lot of conflicting opinions about the best time to put a baby on the pot, but we are firm believers in the regular after-meal session. (After-breakfast, in our case, has been particularly fruitful.)

The chances of hitting the jackpot are not necessarily any greater, but you can make very good use of the time by carrying out the burping drill (which in itself has been known to encourage bigger and better things). Tempting though it may be to skip this routine when you're in a rush or short of patience, and boring though it is, stick to it. If it only saves three messy diapers a week, it's worth the effort.

Occasionally and quite accidentally in the early stages, the enforced period on the pot will coincide with a bowel movement. Your natural reaction is to breathe a sigh of relief, put a fresh diaper on your baby, and get on with the business of the day. Before you do, it's well worth spending a couple of moments on what will at first strike you as a rather curious ritual.

Babies find their feces fascinating, and they love applause. You can profit from these two chinks in their armor. Every time something does actually appear in the pot, show your baby

(who will be very intrigued), and offer loud and prolonged congratulations. You never know. With some babies, flattery is sometimes stronger than the will to win. If your baby is susceptible, it could speed up the toilet-training period considerably.

Having lulled you into thinking that you're making progress, your baby will probably counterattack with an infuriating rearguard action. After a long and totally unproductive session on the pot, you give up and change the diaper. Almost within seconds, you are made aware by either loud yells or the broadest of grins that what was hoped for earlier has suddenly come to pass. Your baby is smelly but triumphant.

There's no way of preventing this trick every time it's attempted, but there are certain signals that usually precede the event. Here they are:

● A sudden period of silence and a preoccupied air.

- A gradual sidling move towards a corner, or behind a piece of furniture. This is not a wholesome desire for privacy; it's an attempt at concealment until the deed is safely done.
- If no natural cover is available, the brazen approach is sometimes used, right out in the open. The only giveaway here is a set look to the mouth and a glassy, faraway stare.

With practice, you'll come to recognize these signs, and have time to take defensive action.

The Search for a Perfect Pot

Ideally, a pot should be solid enough to foil attempts to overturn it, and comfortable enough to accommodate the passenger for extended periods of time without causing cramp or bruising. As optional extras, a seat belt and arm rests would be useful.

Unfortunately, bulk and cost make the production of such a design unlikely, so you'll have to make do with the imperfect models that are currently available. Look for a pot with a thick rim (sitting on a narrow rim is agony) and a broad base. The kind which has a shield over the front part is excellent if your baby is a boy; boys are much less tidy and accurate when urinating than are girls.

Don't confuse the issue with a pot that looks like a duck or a dog or a flying saucer. Don't send a toy to do a pot's job. Toilet training is not a game; it's a serious business.

Asking for the Bathroom

Keep it short and simple. One word is better than a phrase, and a short word is better than a long one. Judged by these criteria, plain old "Pot" is hard to beat.

Walking and Other Dangerous Pastimes

For the first six months or so, your opponent has been confined to areas of your choosing and has been unable to escape. Alas, the rules are about to change drastically. You will find that crawling, stumbling, staggering, lurching and falling over are added to your baby's capabilities. The enemy is now mobile. It's the end of trench warfare and the beginning of guerilla work.

(One small consolation is that there's nothing like a brisk crawl to reduce a baby to a state of healthy and cooperative exhaustion. Take advantage of any large open spaces to slip the leash and let the crawler crawl.)

Obviously, the biggest change you have to face is that your baby no longer has to fight you on your own ground. Instead, you'll face organized resistance in carefully chosen spots where you are particularly vulnerable—places where threat of serious injury or expensive damage can bring you to your knees.

It would be nice if there were some way of teaching your baby what not to touch, what not to do, and where not to go without your constantly saying no. This is boring for both of you, but we haven't heard of any other way that works. Teaching that certain objects, areas, and actions are forbidden is a tedious business requiring nonstop attention and so many no's that you begin to sound like a nagging parrot.

You can keep this down to a minimum by child-proofing forbidden areas along the lines we suggest, but you can't avoid it altogether. Don't forget that your baby wants your attention and is prepared to put up with a few no's to get it.

Here is a selection of the more popular spots for an ambush, and some precautions to take before it's too late:

Stairs

The favored position is baby at the top and you at the bottom. This forces you to creep very slowly up the stairs, arms outstretched, flinching at every unsteady movement, until you reach the top step. Your baby will then laugh in your face, wait until you're safely out of the way, and do it again. It always works.

To prevent this humiliating performance, fix wooden gates at each end of the staircase. (Get the expanding kind of gate and you can also use them to block off open doors and passageways.) Or you can always teach your baby to negotiate the stairs alone. To get down, crawling backwards is best for beginners, and a few demonstrations by you is all it takes for the lesson to sink in. However, bear in mind that crawling down stairs is no fun at all compared with the pleasure of watching you panic, so don't expect this new game to be as effective as the wooden gates.

Coffee Tables

These pieces of furniture—particularly the ones with marble or glass tops—could have been specially designed to worry you. The edges are sharp, the objects on top are easily accessible, and the height is perfect for the baby who likes to crawl underneath and then threaten to stand up and get a concussion. What can you do?

A bolt high up on the living room door will solve the problem altogether. If you feel you can't seal off the living room, you can disarm the coffee table to a certain extent by clearing the top completely and by taping foam rubber padding round the sharp edges and corners. This style is known as Infant Provincial. One

look at it, and you may prefer to hide the coffee table away in the closet for a couple of years until the danger period passes.

Kitchens

The kitchen is more dangerous, and thus more fascinating to babies, than any other room in the house. For the mechanically minded, there are gas stoves and electric grills, micro-wave ovens and food processors; for the adventurous gourmet, there are dozens of brightly colored and attractive packages and bottles containing everything from Liquid Joy to Drano. Disaster lurks at every level and in every corner.

Putting the kitchen totally out of bounds is impractical, and making it totally safe is impossible. All you can do is make sure you never leave your baby in there alone, and develop safety habits such as locking all low-level closets, or keeping them clear of lethal products; always turning pot handles inward on the stove; and unplugging all appliances when you're not using them.

If you think these are obvious precautions to take, look at the accident statistics relating to babies and kitchens. The casualty rate would be a lot lower if everybody showed some common sense.

Electric Sockets

All babies, at one time or another, have ambitions to electrify themselves. Signs to watch out for are two fingers extended in the plug position, and a persistent interest in wires and switches. Before this interest becomes fatal, get plenty of plug blanks for the sockets, and staple or tape all wiring firmly in place along the wall.

Bathrooms

The classic bathroom caper goes something like this. You hear the bathroom door slam. Silence. You rush to the door and find it locked. You hear the sound of running water. Your efforts to get in become frenzied; you find it difficult to kick the door down and speak in a calm and soothing voice at the same time. You hear a thump, followed by crying. The sound of running water continues. You call the neighbors, the police, and the fire department. The baby is finally rescued, damp but victorious, having succeeded in bringing six adults to the brink of cardiac arrest.

There is only one way to prevent this nightmare: Fix a bolt high up on the outside of the bathroom door and *use it religiously.* And keep all poisons, medications and glass bottles in the upper cabinet for *at least* the first five years.

Other People's Homes

Babies love to go visiting. The minute you arrive in a friend's house—or better still, a stranger's—the alert baby senses that you are sitting on the edge of your chair. Here in neutral territory, the two of you are on more or less equal terms; neither of you knows the geography of the house, or where the best places are to mount an ambush. The difference is that your baby will be searching them out while you are trying to socialize. With this serious handicap facing you every time you go visiting, it's worth asking yourself if the journey is really necessary. If it is, take plenty of toys and plenty of spare diapers, and keep those eyes in the back of your head wide open.

Sports Section

Experts on rearing children tell us about the educational benefits of game-playing. They're right, of course. Whether it's learning to walk or learning to count, the more fun it is for the child, the quicker you see results.

We are fond of games for a different and far less noble reason; games can reduce babies to a state of obedient exhaustion. For once, nature is on your side. You're heavier, faster, better coordinated, and you have a longer reach. As long as you use these advantages ruthlessly, you're bound to win more often than you lose.

Games, toys, and other pieces of equipment will need to change with the various stages and ages your baby goes through, so the guide that follows is broken down by age groups.

They're only approximate ages, and our listing of games is by no means comprehensive, but it will at least give you a few ideas. The Exhaustion Rating we give each game is very, very general; individual levels of patience, stamina, and imagination differ so much that it would be impossible to provide more than a rough indication of the degree of exhaustion you can hope to achieve with each game.

Come out fighting when the bell sounds, and good luck.

Strictly for Beginners

AGE	GAME	EQUIPMENT	EXHAUSTION RATING
0—6 months	*Back-pedaling*. Place baby on back. Grasp feet and "bicycle" the legs vigorously. Alternate between fast and slow. For some reason, babies find changes of speed hilarious. The resulting laughter is good exercise for their stomach muscles. *Arm Wrestling*. Same principle, but you hold onto the hands instead of the feet and use a push-pull motion instead of bicycling. *Finger-catching*. Hold your index finger about a foot away from the baby's face, and move it slowly from side to side. Allow your finger to be caught at least as often as it escapes.	You.	Excellent. A few minutes of this three-part program two or three times a day is enough to wear any baby out. Note: not to be played when baby's stomach is full.

Tactics for Toddlers

AGE	GAME	EQUIPMENT	EXHAUSTION RATING
6—9 months	*Fetchit*. A favorite with most babies. It consists of throwing things out of the crib or high chair and yelling until you pick them up. You can counter this tiresome tactic by tying toys to crib or chair with a short piece of elastic so that they bounce back when thrown.	A selection of most-liked small toys, and some strong elastic.	Poor.
	Bouncing. The investment required (see equipment) is well worth it. You can hang the bouncer from any convenient doorway, so that you and baby can still see each other. It's safe, it needs little effort from you, and it's very tiring for your baby. Who could ask for anything more?	A doorway swing—a sit-in harness that you hang from the door frame with thick elastic ropes.	Terrific. Half an hour of this is as effective as going fifteen rounds with Ali would be for you or me.

Tactics for Toddlers

AGE	GAME	EQUIPMENT	EXHAUSTION RATING
6—9 months	*Minor Chaos.* This age loves undoing, unscrewing, and emptying. No drawer, box or shelf is safe unless you provide plenty of more attractive alternatives.	Boxes with lids, jars with tops. Fill them with small toys or household objects, like teaspoons, that are unbreakable and too big to swallow.	Untidy, and not very tiring, but excellent diversion.

For the More Advanced

AGE	GAME	EQUIPMENT	EXHAUSTION RATING
9—18 months	*Scooting*. Played at ever-increasing speeds as legs and coordination develop. Seated in a walker (see Equipment), your baby will be happy for extended periods of time whizzing around like an overwound clockwork toy. Tie a few small playthings—a rattle, a doll, a plastic hammer—to the walker, and encourage maximum mileage.	The standard four-wheel walker with heavy-duty canvas cockpit. Get a good sturdy one; the lightweight racing models tend to fall apart after a few weeks.	Wonderful. We have seen many babies scoot themselves into a docile trance caused by fatigue and enjoyment.

For the More Advanced

AGE	GAME	EQUIPMENT	EXHAUSTION RATING
9—18 months	*Getting under Your Feet.* There is a certain age, usually around one year, when all your baby really wants to do is follow you around the house. This often coincides with those first uncertain attempts at walking and navigation, so progress is never fast and sometimes painful. You are constantly having to pick up and comfort a small screeching figure who has been attacked by a piece of furniture or tripped up by a rug.	It helps if your baby has something to hang onto while walking. A small cart is probably best, but anything stable and on wheels will do.	High, for both of you. Your longer legs and superior housecraft will eventually outlast your opponent, but it's a tiring business.

Playing Alone

From the age of just a few weeks, your baby will happily play alone if there is something fascinating enough to play with. It's hardly something you can teach, but it's certainly something you can encourage. Here are a few hints you may find useful in nudging your baby into the habit.

- Check the reaction to various types of toy. Babies differ in their toy tastes just as adults differ in their tastes in books or sports. Some babies love puzzles or mechanical toys; other babies find these frustrating and are happier with books or blocks. You can only find out by trial and error, but you'll see a preference emerge quite quickly.
- Don't hover. You obviously have to keep an eye on your baby, but do it from a distance. Otherwise, you will become essential to the act of playing.
- By and large, the most successful and enduring toys are the old standbys like balls, rings, blocks, and robust push-pull toys. Get the best quality you can find. Toys that break easily can make a baby feel clumsy and guilty. Don't despair if there are days when nothing will do except you. And don't get upset when, on other days, your company is spurned in favor of a plastic frog or a bucket of mud.

A Cure for Combat Fatigue

ired? Irritable? Prone to homicidal tendencies? Does the sight of a diaper make you wince?

You're not sick; you're just fed up. Most new parents feel exactly like that after the first few weeks of parenthood. They've had an overdose of baby, and they need a break.

As a general and completely arbitrary rule, you should have one day or evening away from your baby each week. And it should be a *rule*. Time off is good for you, good for your marriage, and good for your baby. (Sooner or later, the baby's got to get used to other faces besides yours. Why not sooner?)

The younger a baby is when you start going out, the less chance there is of a tantrum. If you wait until your baby is old enough to grasp the principle of baby-sitting before you go out for an evening, you'll have a long wait. Take the plunge. You'll find that babies who are regularly left with sitters soon accept them as part of their lives.

Admittedly, finding a good sitter isn't always easy. If you're lucky, you'll already know someone in the neighborhood, or your friends will be able to recommend one. If not, you'll have to make a choice based on a very brief acquaintance. And since there are no diplomas given out for trusty and qualified sitters, you'll be forced to rely on your instincts.

Test #1: Would you trust the prospective sitter with your car, an important message, cash, or your front door key? If not, you certainly won't feel happy trusting her with your baby.

Test #2: Before you make up your mind, introduce prospective sitter to baby. A few minutes watching the two of them together will tell you a lot.

Once you find a good sitter you'll want to hang on to her. The following do's and don'ts worked very well for us in avoiding misunderstandings and maintaining an amiable working relationship.

- Have the sitter come fifteen or twenty minutes before you want to leave, so you can show her what she needs to see in the house. Even after she becomes familiar with the house, the extra fifteen minutes will come in handy to bring her up to date on the baby's latest bedtime idiosyncrasies.

- Establish the rate in advance. Haggling over money at 1 a.m. is a dismal way to end an evening.

- Make it a firm rule that your sitter does not entertain visitors. It's a paid job, not an excuse for a party.

- Leave a list of all important phone numbers by the phone. If you find that the number where you can be reached that evening is not the one you left on your list, call home with the new number.

- Leave detailed written instructions if the baby will need to be fed or given medication while you're out.

- Don't expect sitters to do dishes or housework. That's not what you're paying them for.

- Give your sitter the spare pacifier or magic blanket in case of loss or emergency.

- Be punctual yourself. When you say you're going to be back by midnight, it isn't fair to roll in at 2 a.m. If you're going to be later than you thought, call home with the new time.

There is always the possibility that you won't need to worry about recruiting sitters. You may have a source of unlimited free sitting talent not too far away—the grandparents.

Opinions are sharply divided on the merits of grandparents as sitters. They're free, and usually delighted to help. They know you, the baby and the house. And you trust them.

On the other hand, there is often a problem that has been described as the "we know best" syndrome. Having reared you with such extraordinary success, your parents will tend to apply their ideas and techniques to the rearing of their grandchild. This may not suit you. If it doesn't, be prepared for some awkward moments.

You might like the sound of a compromise system, which has worked well for several couples we know. Weekdays, you hire sitters; weekends, you drop the baby off with grandparents. Try it out. In fact, try it out this weekend. It's never too soon to start.

1. Historic Moments

Baby came out fighting on
_____

Moved out of hospital and
invaded home on
_____

Committed first tactical error by sleeping
through the entire night on
_____

Retaliated by cutting first tooth
very noisily on
_____

Abandoned crawling in favor of
two-legged maneuvers on
_____

Escaped from crib on
_____

Issued first verbal command on
_____

2. Vital Phone Numbers

Police:
_____

Doctor:
_____

Fire Department:
_____

Liquor Store:
_____

Baby Sitter:
_____

Plumber:
_____

Locksmith:
_____